Copyright © 1993 Creative Editions.
123 South Broad Street, Mankato, MN 56001, USA
International copyrights reserved in all countries. No part of this book may
be reproduced in any form without written permission from the publisher.
Printed in Italy
Art Director: Rita Marshall
Book Design: Stephanie Blumenthal
Text Adapted and Edited from the French language by Kitty Benedict
Library of Congress Cataloging-in-Publication Data
Benedict, Kitty.
Air/written by Andrienne Soutter-Perrot; adapted for the American reader
by Kitty Benedict; illustrated by Etienne Delessert.
Summary: Discusses the physical properties and the importance of air.
ISBN 1-56846-037-6
1. Air—Juvenile literature. [1. Air.]
I. Soutter-Perrot, Andrienne. II. Delessert, Etienne, ill. III. Title.
QC161.2.B45 1992
533'.6--dc20   92-5071

AIR

WRITTEN BY

ANDRIENNE SOUTTER-PERROT

ILLUSTRATED BY

ETIENNE DELESSERT

CREATIVE EDITIONS

WHAT DOES AIR LOOK LIKE?

What color is the air? What shape is it? Does it look like any of the shapes above?

Does it look like a rock, or a tree, or a cloud, or a rabbit?

Air is everywhere, all around us, but we cannot see the air because it is invisible.

Air has no shape, but it fills everything. Air is everywhere, even in the things that look empty.

Although air is invisible and has no shape, you can see its strength on a windy day.

You can feel its force when you ride your bike.

WHAT DOES AIR WEIGH?

Air is everywhere we go on Earth, even on
the highest mountain.

Air surrounds the entire planet. This blanket of air covering the
Earth is called the atmosphere.

Although the atmosphere is very large, the air that it is made up of feels like it has no weight.

But in fact, air does weigh something. A liter of air weighs just a little more than one gram, which is about the same as a single pea.

And taken together, all the air around the Earth weighs very much.
This weight constantly presses down on the Earth's surface and is
called "atmospheric pressure."

WHAT IS AIR MADE OF?

Air is a mixture of gases, including nitrogen, oxygen, carbon dioxide, and water vapor. The most important part of air for humans is the gas called oxygen.

Like all gases, air can take many different forms. When you blow air into a balloon, you are squeezing, or compressing, the air to fill the balloon.

If you compress air hard enough, you can pack a lot of air into a small space.

Air also has other unique qualities. When it is made very, very cold,
it eventually turns into a liquid.

−200°C −360°F

If this liquid is made even colder, it turns into a solid block.

WHY DO WE NEED AIR?

Lie very still for a moment. Take a deep breath and then let it out. Do you feel your chest moving in and out?

Your chest moves because you are breathing air into your body and then pushing it out.

When you breathe in, the oxygen in the air passes into your lungs.
From there it goes to all the cells in your body. Your body needs
oxygen to stay alive.

When you breathe out, or exhale, you get rid of the gas called
carbon dioxide.

All kinds of animals need to breathe. Plants need to breathe, too.

It is important to keep our air clean and free of harmful gases.

WHERE DOES AIR COME FROM?

Each green plant and tree is like a little factory for making oxygen.

These little oxygen factories work only during the day, because they need sunlight to make oxygen.

Many plants and trees grouped together form a large and powerful oxygen-making factory.

All green plants and trees absorb water, oxygen, and carbon dioxide from the air. Then they convert the water and carbon dioxide into more oxygen. This process is called photosynthesis.

In this way plants and trees help to clean the air we breathe.

Without clean and healthy air we could not live.